Original title:
Soil and Sonnets

Copyright © 2025 Creative Arts Management OÜ
All rights reserved.

Author: Christian Leclair
ISBN HARDBACK: 978-1-80566-628-8
ISBN PAPERBACK: 978-1-80566-913-5

## Fertile Lines of Love

In a garden where laughter grows,
Worms wiggle in their Sunday clothes.
A carrot dreams of being a star,
While radishes giggle in the jar.

Bees stage buzzers, a melodic choir,
Petals dance in a floral attire.
With every seed that goes to bed,
A joke is told by the leafy head.

## Nature's Stanza

Dandelions plot their grand escape,
Wishing for crowns in a royal shape.
Ants play tag on a blade of grass,
While butterflies check their mirrored glass.

The trees hold meetings, branches sway,
Sharing secrets of the sunny day.
A squirrel rehearses his stand-up show,
While mushrooms giggle beneath the glow.

## Tilling the Heart's Canvas

We dig and delve with shovels bright,
Uncovering treasures that sparkle in light.
Onions cry from the laughter below,
While potatoes snicker, putting on a show.

With trowels in hand, we cultivate cheer,
Pansies chuckle as we draw near.
A tomato winks, ripe and round,
In this patch of joy, humor's found.

## **Subterranean Rhymes**

Deep in the earth, where roots do play,
A drama unfolds in the mud each day.
The turnips gossip, the beets all grin,
As the underground crew spins tales of sin.

Worms recite poems of squishy delight,
While mushrooms giggle throughout the night.
Each laugh in the dark spreads seeds of cheer,
Growing joy in the soil, year after year.

## Pondering the Undergrowth

In the garden where weeds play,
A gnome in ballet shoes sway,
Worms do the cha-cha in rows,
While the daisies gossip and dose.

Rabbits discuss politics there,
Their ears like antennas in air,
"Oh, to be a carrot," one cried,
"It's safer underground," he sighed.

## **The Rooted Dreamscape**

Underneath where the weird roots twist,
Fairies have a tiny bar on a mist,
They mix drinks with dew drops and cheer,
"Who needs the sun? We thrive down here!"

Dancing mushrooms don their sleek hats,
Toasting to slugs and their business chats,
"I swear this mold gives me a high!"
"The secret is patience, oh my oh my!"

**Lyrical Landscapes**

A farmer sings to his crop of peas,
"Dance, my little veggies, with ease!"
The carrots reply with a chuckle and grin,
"Watch us wiggle! Let the fun begin!"

On a potato, a beet does a jig,
While a tomato dreams of being big,
"Let's make a salad, squeeze some lime,"
"Only if it's our in-season prime!"

## **Strains of the Substrate**

In the depths where the critters convene,
A concert of roots plays a quirky scene,
A beetle strums on a leaf lute,
While a snail keeps time, what a hoot!

"Let's start a band," calls a bold ant,
"We'll rock the underground, oh what a chant!"
But oops! A toad hops in the way,
"Quiet down, you rascals, I'm trying to play!"

## The Palette of Planting

In the garden where veggies dance,
A carrot twirls, takes a chance.
The tomatoes giggle, red as can be,
While the radishes shout, "Look at me!"

Potatoes get lazy, buried so deep,
Dreaming of chips, counting sheep.
The beans climb high, thinking they're cool,
But keep tripping over their own little spool.

The lettuce is crisp, but oh so shy,
While pickles just pickle on the sly.
Insects hold parties, buzzing with glee,
Declaring, "Who knew we could live so free!"

Amidst all the chaos, a worm takes a ride,
Laughing at all, he's the wiggling pride.
As bees sip nectar from flowers so bright,
The garden's a stage, what a comical sight!

**Verses Woven in Roots**

In the meadow where laughter grows wide,
Critters and flowers all take a stride.
The daisies debate who smells the best,
While the sunflowers play 'who's tallest?' quest.

A grasshopper croaks in a karaoke show,
To crickets who hop, putting on a glow.
The daisies can't follow the tricky tune,
While the butterfly whispers, "You'll get it by noon!"

The mushrooms have secrets, giggling so loud,
Poking their heads from the leafy crowd.
The ants march in step, looking quite grand,
While the frogs time their jumps, life's high demand.

Caught in this chaos, a little bird sneaks,
He dreams big dreams of far-away peaks.
In the tapestry of giggles, nature's delight,
Every wiggle, every giggle, feels just right!

**Unseen Nurture**

In the garden of dreams, seeds play hide and seek,
With worms on a mission, making their sneak peek.
Dandelions laugh, as daisies take flight,
The sun says, 'Get growing!' while stars share their light.

Rabbits in bow ties are having a ball,
While broccoli dances and peas have a ball.
The carrots are gossiping, 'Did you see that?'
While radishes wink under their green, leafy hat.

## The Harvest of Words

With quills made of clovers, and ink from the dew,
Words sprout like daisies, surprising me and you.
Puns bloom like flowers, with petals of cheer,
As laughter grows louder, we draw near.

Sentences wiggle, like worms in the sun,
Verbs play tag, and adjectives run.
Nobody knows where the commas will lie,
But every pause is a chance to fly.

## Rhapsody of the Wild

The critters conduct a symphony there,
With crickets on violins and rabbits that share.
A chorus of frogs in a big muddy pond,
Compose tunes so silly, of which we're all fond.

The fox wears a top hat, the owl is the lead,
While squirrels form a band with acorns to seed.
They strum on the branches, they dance all around,
In this wild serenade, joy endlessly found.

## Beneath the Surface

Underneath the chaos, there's laughter so low,
As beetles hold meetings where secrets can grow.
The ants in the tunnel are working in rhyme,
Building their cities, one sandwich at a time.

Moles play hide and seek, while snails leave a trail,
Worms write the stories in loops like a snail.
Each wiggle and jiggle, a comedy reel,
In the depths of the earth, the humor's quite real.

# Roots Run Deep

In the garden where gnomes dance,
Chasing worms in a wild prance,
The roots chuckle beneath the ground,
Whispering secrets, silly sounds.

A carrot jokes with a brave old beet,
'Your orange looks better in the heat!'
While radishes roll with laughter bright,
Under the moon's soft, joke-telling light.

The flowers gossip with petals wide,
'Is that a weed, or am I dignified?'
They twirl and sway, in playful delight,
Creating mischief all through the night.

## Colors of the Underworld

Oh, the hues beneath our feet so sly,
Dirt so rich, it makes the worms fly,
The fungi wear hats, wide and grand,
While the rocks gossip, forming a band.

Glowing greens and browns, what a sight!
The roots are a disco, grooving all night,
"Let's paint the earth!" they cheer and shout,
As earthworms wiggle without a doubt.

From dusty gray to a muddy brown,
Colors burst forth like a jester's gown,
The underground party, a joke-filled shout,
Who knew the depths could turn inside out?

## **Lyrical Landscape**

In the field where daisies prance,
The grass sings songs of charm and chance,
A lyrical laugh from morning dew,
Tickles the roots in a funny view.

The breeze hums notes of a sweet refrain,
While bushes pout, playing coy in vain,
"Why can't we dance?" a shrublet cries,
As beetles twirl 'neath the sunny skies.

A symphony weaves through nature's roof,
Wondering if it's fact or spoof,
Each petal, each leaf, a note to share,
Creating music in the warm, soft air.

## A Tapestry of Time

Threads of laughter stitched in dirt,
A tapestry where mishaps flirt,
Bulbous goodbyes and leafy hellos,
In this world where humor grows.

Each layer tells a tale of yore,
Where a snail's race is never a bore,
"Catch me if you can!" a tortoise teases,
While the daisies giggle, swaying with breezes.

With every season, a comic plot,
Where fields get wild with a wink and a thought,
Time wraps around in a playful brawl,
Creating a fabric that binds us all.

## **Porcelain Petals**

In a garden, the flowers wear dresses,
A daisy is twirling, causing some messes.
A tulip took a trip, got lost in the sun,
While the roses just giggled—oh, what silly fun!

The bees think they're dancers, buzz in a line,
Waltzing through blossoms with moves so divine.
The gardener sighs, with dirt on his nose,
Says, "All this excitement, where did it come from? Who knows!"

## Songs of the Thicket

A rabbit with rhythm hops on the beat,
With squirrels performing in tap shoes, oh sweet!
The hedgehogs hum softly, start a new craze,
While the owls just wonder through bemused gaze.

When the fox joins in, wearing shades of bright red,
The dance floors erupt, foliage swayed with dread.
Each creature a star in this woodland delight,
As critters come together in the soft moonlight.

## The Breath of Growth

Tiny seeds hold parties, sprouting with cheer,
Chattering and laughing, nothing to fear.
They poke through the ground, pushing up new heads,
Wondering if they'll turn into something that spreads.

The worms are the DJs, turning beats of the earth,
While ladybugs gossip of all that it's worth.
Each leaf is a dancer, shaking in the sun,
While grass tips its hat—oh, this is so much fun!

## Harmonies Beneath the Trowel

The shovel sings softly with a musical tone,
As it digs through the earth, carving out its own zone.
The rake hums along, with a sweep and a swish,
Creating a symphony, oh what a dish!

In the patch where the carrots grow wild and free,
The radishes gossip as they sip herbal tea.
With laughter and joy beneath the blue sky,
Even the potatoes wink, "Oh me, oh my!"

## In the Clutch of Clay

Muddy hands and happy cries,
Worms wiggling, oh what a surprise!
Planting seeds and making bets,
Who knew gardening comes with sweats?

With every weed, a joke is spun,
A flower's bloom is purest fun!
Digging deep with sticks and twine,
Laughing hard with friends divine.

**Poetic Gardens Unfurled**

In the garden, plants collide,
A chubby rabbit tries to hide.
He munches carrots, wide-eyed glee,
While bees buzz by in harmony.

Nonsense blooms, in every hue,
Petunias giggle, can you too?
Tomatoes dance, the cucumbers prance,
Together they join in a funny dance.

## Beneath the Boughs of Emotion

Silly squirrels throw acorns high,
The branches shake, a playful sigh.
Beneath the shade, the laughter peals,
A picnic spread with funny meals.

A sandwich smiles, a cookie grins,
Nature's joy where laughter begins.
With every bite and every cheer,
Life in the trees is bright and clear.

## The Richness of the Undercurrent

Underfoot, the critters scurry,
Ants in line, they're never blurry.
Fungi giggle, mosses sigh,
What a world beneath, oh my!

In every corner, a secret plot,
A cackle here, a chuckle not.
With roots that twist and tales that weave,
The underground's a place to believe.

## Earth's Embrace

In a garden where carrots giggle,
Tomatoes blush while dancing a jig.
The earth's warm hug feels like a tickle,
Even worms wear shades, looking big!

As plants tell jokes beneath the sun,
The daisies laugh, oh what a scene!
With every sprout, the fun has begun,
Life in the dirt is quite the routine!

Squirrels challenge potatoes to races,
While bees buzz in comical flight.
The daisies play poker, showing their faces,
And ants march home, proud of their bite!

In this land where humor can thrive,
With roots that tangle in playful delight.
Let's join the jest; we're all alive,
In the embrace of nature, we take flight!

## **Verses of the Ground**

Underfoot lies a world so silly,
Where mushrooms wear hats like strange old men.
Worms play jazz, making everyone frilly,
And crickets form bands with a cheer and then!

The daisies debate who's the fairest,
While grasshoppers juror with laughter as law.
The rocks tell tales, quite the rarest,
As the squirrel judges with a pensive paw.

We dance with weeds, our partners in crime,
Twirling and swirling in glorious spins.
Nature's oddities flex their prime,
Celebrating life with all its whims!

In verses down low, the humor is rich,
As laughter and roots weave stories anew.
Each little creature adds just a stitch,
In the narrative where silliness grew!

## **Whispering Roots**

Beneath the surface, secrets unwind,
Where chatter grows thick in the dirt's embrace.
Roots gossip tales that tickle the mind,
While ladybugs prance with a comical grace.

Twisting and turning, they share funny dreams,
Of flowers that wear mismatched shoes.
The pebbles chuckle, or so it seems,
At the antics of ants with their glittering ruse!

A thistle cracks jokes, sharp yet sly,
While shadows of leaves offer whispers of fun.
In this realm where nature can fly,
Humor blooms bright under the warm sun!

So come join the giggle beneath your feet,
Where the underground parties are always a treat.
In the realm of the roots, life's never discreet,
And in every corner, there's laughter so sweet!

## Melodies Beneath

Giggles and whispers rise from below,
As flowers sway to nature's strange tune.
A playful parade of green on the go,
Under the light of the chuckling moon.

The beetles, they sing with a raucous cheer,
While daisies provide the perfect backup band.
In harmonies danced, they've nothing to fear,
A cacophony made by the fun-loving land!

With roots that entangle, they form quite a crew,
As mischief unfolds on the earthen stage.
Each insect a dancer, each plant a debut,
This earthy ensemble never shows rage!

So listen closely to this merry sound,
In the realm where laughter and life intertwine.
Melodies bright springing up from the ground,
In a world where the funny holds the divine!

## Cultivating Dreams

I planted a seed with a hope and a laugh,
It sprouted a shoe, now I'm part of the craft.
The garden looks odd, with its fashion gone rogue,
My veggies wear hats; it's a whimsical vogue.

The carrots are dancing, the beets play in bands,
The lettuce is laughing, they're all holding hands.
But when it rains hard, what a slippery scene,
My garden's a circus, quite wacky and keen.

Fertilizer's flying, the weeds throw a feast,
They called for my help, but I'm not the least.
I'd rather have worms sing a tune in the sun,
Than fight for my patch; oh, this madness is fun!

The tomatoes are gossiping, full of sweet lore,
They dream of a stage, and they practice encore.
My patch is a joke, that I tend with a grin,
Cultivating laughter, where the fun must begin.

## Sanctity of the Patch

In my sacred garden, there's chaos abound,
The radishes shout, and the onions fall down.
I trip on a trowel, the rake gives a spin,
It's a dance of the plants, and I'm dragged right in.

The peas form a line, in a vegetable band,
With broccoli strumming while carrots make stand.
The wells of their laughter bubble up through the roots,
My patch is a party, with gardens in toots.

Each flower is pointing, with petals in glee,
As I try to focus on trimmings and tea.
But every time I bend, they burst into song,
It's a turf of tomfoolery, nothing feels wrong.

So here in this jocund, most sacred of places,
I find joy in the weeds, and give gloomy faces,
A sanctuary thrives, with my friends in the ground,
Where laughter and chaos are inherently found.

## Petals in the Wind

The petals are spinning like tops in the breeze,
They swirl with such fervor, it's hard not to tease.
I thought they were flowers, discussing haute trends,
But they're gossiping petals, just making amends.

I chased them around, like a dog with a tail,
As they frolicked and danced, leaving sparkle and trail.
They painted my garden in colors so bright,
In a whirl of their laughter, they light up the night.

The daisies are critiquing the tulips' new look,
While sunflowers wink, oh what a silly book!
It's a bloom full of joy in this jovial sphere,
With petals that flutter; they banter and cheer.

As I laugh away worries in this floral parade,
I sigh, what a pastime, this outing I've made.
For joy in the journey brings mirth in the blend,
Who knew that the flowers could also be friends?

## Melancholy of the Clay

Oh, the mud is a maven, it seems full of woe,
It grabs at my boots, like a toddler's wild show.
In a pit with my spade, I struggle and sigh,
As the earth giggles softly, watching me try.

It cloaks me in laughter, with each slip and trip,
My dignity buried, can't manage a grip.
The pigeons in chorus poke fun at my plight,
While I dig for my pride, out of sight from their sight.

The gopher seems puzzled; he pokes out his head,
As I wade through this goo, wishing to be fed.
But the clay throws a party, in all of its grief,
It's a muddy mischief, so laugh 'til belief.

As I roll in the muck, I find joy in the mess,
At least I'm not lonely, with my dirt-ridden dress.
For when life gets too heavy, a tumble can clear,
And dancing with clay is the best kind of cheer.

## The Pulse of the Undergrowth

In the garden where gophers play,
The carrots plot their great escape.
Worms do tango in the clay,
While daisies giggle and reshape.

Ants march in a goofy line,
With breadcrumbs like their golden prize.
They'll dance all day and sip on brine,
While sunbeams tease them with surprise.

A frog sings off-key every night,
Chorusing with crickets for fame.
The moon chuckles at this delight,
And all join in the silly game.

On summer days, the beetles race,
A snail's got tricks, he coaches slow.
Their antics put us in a daze,
As they argue where the best grass grows.

## In Praise of Earthbound Echoes

Beneath the surface, secrets swirl,
A mouse in boots wants to be king.
He twirls around a muddy whirl,
While daisies laugh at everything.

The clouds above just scratch their heads,
Pigeons gossip with the trees.
Oh, those playful, floppy spreads,
Spreading dirt without a tease.

With every quake, a worm's lament,
As mushrooms take their evening stroll.
They claim the throne with content,
While bugs hold parties in a bowl.

And in this realm of roots and grime,
We find a dance of pure delight.
For there's humor in the rhyme,
Of laughter echoed through the night.

## Unwritten Tales of the Ground

Once a pebble had a dream,
It wanted more than just to lay.
To be a star, or so it seemed,
Yet rolled away and lost its way.

A beetle wrote a bestseller,
His neighbor thought it quite absurd.
With finest lines and hidden cellar,
All the ants agreed, it was a word.

There's chatter 'round the onions bright,
About the tales of buried mute.
An old worm swears he'll get it right,
If only he could find a root.

The drama thrives beneath the grass,
Each whisper brings a grin or snare.
From tiny seeds that slowly amass,
To mighty tales that float through air.

## Cantos of the Cradle

In the cradle of the brownish hue,
Racers sprint and tumble true.
A toad croaks out a jest or two,
While timid squirrels learn to moo.

The mighty oak claims lofty airs,
But it's a jester at heart,
As kittens hide in leafy lairs,
And everyone plays a part.

The ladybugs perform a play,
While tiny roots compose the score.
With every squabble through the day,
They tickle grasses evermore.

And as the stars begin to peek,
The chatter fades to sleepy sighs.
In cuddled nooks and shadows meek,
The joy of silliness survives.

## Flourish in the Dark

Beneath the earth where secrets lie,
The worms have parties, oh my, oh my!
With tiny hats and dance so spry,
They groove to tunes we can't deny.

The daisies whisper, 'What a show!'
With roots that wiggle, stealing the glow.
To the rhythm of the mystic flow,
They twirl and leap, all in a row.

When night descends, they laugh out loud,
While moles pick up the crickets' crowd.
In shadows deep, they form a shroud,
Embracing fun, they feel so proud.

So when you dig and feel the muck,
Remember those who laugh and cluck.
For in the dark, they're all in luck,
Creating joy with every pluck.

## Ode to the Unseen

Oh tiny critters, scurry fast,
In hidden realms where you're amassed.
Your laughter echoes, unsurpassed,
While we above, move quite aghast.

Those beetles boast, 'We'll rule the night!'
With banter sharp and smiles so bright.
They joke of roots that spark delight,
While spinning webs with all their might.

The underground, a merry scene,
Where shadows dance and jesters preen.
Amidst the dirt, they've formed a queen,
In raucous revels, so obscene!

So raise a glass, you on the top,
To laughter's tune, we'll never stop.
For in the depths, the party's pop,
With mischief bold, the crowd will flop.

## **Violin of the Valley**

In valleys low, where mischief thrives,
A squirrel plays, 'What fun!', he jives.
His tiny paws, they dance, they strive,
   To make the roots spin tunes alive.

The grass sings back, its voice a croon,
   While clouds above hum a lazy tune.
With melodies that shake the moon,
   They play till dawn, a vivid boon.

A rabbit joins, his moves quite slick,
   With floppy ears, he does the trick.
Together now, they're quite the clique,
In rhythms bold, they'll dance and kick.

So if you wander, hear this lore,
Of unseen joys and melodies galore.
In valleys green, they laugh and soar,
Where nature's whimsy opens the door.

## Phrases in the Furrow

Out in the field, where laughter grows,
The seeds can chat as everyone knows.
With puns and jests, they steal the show,
In rows of green, their wit just flows.

The carrots chuckle, 'What a day!'
While radishes tease, 'Make way, make way!'
In jestful banter, they gleefully play,
With rhymes that sprout without delay.

The peas declare, 'We're stacked just right,'
With humor sharp, they take their flight.
In friendly jabs, they're full of light,
Turning furrows into pure delight.

So if you pass where laughter's spun,
And hear the whispers of all that's fun,
Know in the ground, the games are won,
As nature smiles beneath the sun.

# The Tapestry of Texture

A worm in a hat laughs, what a sight,
It wiggles and jigs in the warm morning light.
Moles throw a party, they dig and they dance,
In the dark, they're the kings—oh, how they prance!

A patch of tomatoes dreams big and bold,
They wear sun hats to keep from the cold.
Carrots boast wisdom, deep underground,
While radishes giggle without making a sound.

The daisies tell jokes, as bees buzz along,
Quantifying nectar, they hum a sweet song.
Old oak trees chuckle, their branches a sway,
While squirrels are plotting a nut-stealing day!

The roots all connect, gossip thick as a stew,
Each tale more absurd than the last one's review.
This patchwork of life, what craziness here,
Dig deep and you'll see—nature's so dear!

## Subtle Rhythms of the Underfoot

Earthworms are DJs, spinning the beats,
Underground raves with their wiggly feats.
They groove under grass while the daisies inspire,
With roots acting as mics—a botanical choir!

Ants in tuxedos parade to the sound,
Climbing up stems where the thrills can be found.
While beetles conduct, ants march with flair,
Who knew the dark could hold such a rare air?

The crickets compose from dusk until dawn,
While fireflies flash their lights like a con.
And every loud hum from a bumblebee's dron,
Is percussion for flowers that sway all along.

Even puddles get in on this dance-floor affair,
Splashes and splatters, choreographed flair.
It's a whimsical waltz right beneath our feet,
In this lovely abyss, life's rhythms beat sweet!

# **Reflections in Richness**

In the muck, there's humor, watch the frogs rejoice,
With their croaks like opera, they find their own voice.
The mud pies are baking, a chef's wild delight,
While slugs slide on by, giving all a good fright!

Toadstools wear hats, they're the mushrooms of mirth,
Hosting wild parties with worms for their birth.
The grubs tell stories, oh, what a delight,
Adventures unharmed by the sun's glaring light.

Caterpillars wrestle, their fuzz a grand show,
As butterflies flutter, "Oh look at us glow!"
Ladybugs giggle in tuxedos so bright,
Gossiping softly about bugs late at night.

Within this rich banquet, each laugh is a feast,
A celebration of growing, to say the least.
So when you get muddy, let laughter take flight,
For nature's a party both day and by night!

## A Canopy of Cadence

A canopy shimmies; the leaves start to sway,
As squirrels with their acorns go bouncing away.
Chipmunks are hoarding their snacks with great cheer,
Plotting schemes over breakfast, or just the next beer!

A chorus of crows caws high from the trees,
As the breeze takes a giggle through buttons of peas.
The owls hoot in time, wise words they impart,
With a wink, they remind us to laugh from the heart.

The sun tricks the shadows, a game they play cool,
While rabbits race through in a furry, wild school.
It's a sweet, uproarious frolic of life,
Where nature's a stage, free of all strife!

From roots to the branches, let giggles abound,
With whispers and rustles, let joy be found.
So come join the jive under green leafy tents,
In this joyous arena, we'll dance—no regrets!

## A Field of Echoes

In whispered tones the daisies prance,
While garlic sneezes, plants take a chance.
The carrots giggle in their cozy bed,
As radishes argue on who gets fed.

The moon in jest makes shadows leap,
While worms tell tales that make us weep.
A bee hums softly, playing a tune,
While turnips play cards beneath the moon.

Butterflies laugh, and ants come to dance,
Each little life takes a merry stance.
They plot a party on a leafy stage,
In a joyous world, all nature's our age.

Lettuce is winking, potatoes are shy,
Each seedling a dream with a curious eye.
In this playful patch where green dreams blend,
Nature's antics reveal new friends.

## The Hidden Narrative

A tale unfolds beneath the ground,
Where whispering roots make the silliest sound.
The potatoes claim they know all the news,
While peas share secrets as if they could choose.

Carrots tell stories of adventurous bites,
While beets reminisce on their fanciful flights.
Radishes scandalize the gossiping throngs,
With tales of the outsider who just feels wrong.

The grass rolls its eyes at the raucous scenes,
While mushrooms cheer on the dark, sprightly beans.
The daisies snicker, keeping it light,
In this tangled plot where wrong feels just right.

Beneath the coat of nature's attire,
Each tiny critter fuels the choir.
Where laughter sprouts with each growing verse,
And life finds a way to amuse and converse.

## Breaths of the Earth

With each deep breath, the ground gives a snort,
A cabbage makes puns in its leafy court.
The sunflower winks with a golden grin,
While turnips cheer, 'Let the games begin!'

A cozy patch sings with quirky noise,
As seedlings indulge in their playful joys.
The dandelions challenge the clouds up high,
While pumpkins prepare for their party nigh.

The breeze gossips soft, rustling the tales,
Of rabbits whose laughter always prevails.
Each beetroot blushes, shy yet so bold,
As stories of nature's funny unfold.

The earth may be serious, deep, and profound,
Yet here lies the laughter, just waiting around.
With roots in the muck and dreams in the air,
We find in this growth, a reason to share.

## Weaving Growth into Words

In woven threads of green and gold,
Humor sprinkles the stories untold.
Each leaf is a page in this botanical book,
Where broccoli smiles with a playful look.

The cauliflowers dance in silly, round hats,
While dandelions plot against pesky old gnats.
Tomatoes boast of their luscious red hue,
While corn swaps quips with the wise, leafy crew.

Carrots reenact their great swan dive,
As radishes ponder how best to survive.
A patchwork of jokes laid out in the light,
Plants giggling together, oh what a sight!

Each plant contributes to the laughter parade,
In this garden of dreams, a grand masquerade.
Nature's own jester, amusing and spry,
As we weave words and joy by and by.

**Fragments of Flora**

In the garden where weeds hold court,
Veggies plot and tomatoes cavort.
The carrots giggle beneath the dirt,
While turnips wear the sassy shirt.

A radish once tried to lead a dance,
But found it hard to find romance.
With sprouting dreams of being a star,
They tripped and fell; oh how bizarre!

Dandelions laugh, a sprightly crew,
While daisies boast of morning dew.
Each petal tells a tale of glee,
In this wild, leafy comedy.

With bumblebees that buzz in tune,
They hum under the watchful moon.
In this jolly patch where giggles grow,
The plants put on a funny show.

## In the Cradle of Life

Once a seed said, 'I dream to fly!'
A sunflower chortled, 'Oh my, oh my!'
With roots so deep, how could it soar?
They laughed till their leaves were sore.

A worm claimed to be wise and grand,
While munching on a tasty strand.
'You think you're clever,' shouted bean,
'But I'm the one who's truly green!'

The breeze tickled the grass so sweet,
'Trust me,' it whispered, 'you can't be beat!'
While clovers rolled in fits of cheer,
Playing hide and seek with the deer.

In laughter's embrace, all life abounds,
With jokes exchanged from grounds to mounds.
In this cradle where joy takes root,
Every sprout's a comic hoot!

## Poetic Earthworks

With rhythmic roots, the poets sway,
Telling tales of dirt and play.
In rhymes they dig and plant a line,
Creating verses both soft and fine.

A mushroom claimed a spotlight bright,
While sprouting just to share its light.
A toadstool quipped, 'I'm no cliché!'
And danced around in its own way.

A daffodil composed a tune,
Said, 'Life's a laugh, like a cartoon!'
The daisies chimed in harmony,
It's always funny in a spree!

From rich dark loam to skies of blue,
The poets craft with every hue.
In laughter's grain, they find their worth,
These merry minstrels of the earth.

## The Ground Beneath the Penned Sky

Underneath the scribbler's desk,
Lies a realm both weird and grotesque.
With ants in tuxedos, who'd have thought?
Debating how a sandwich's caught?

A rabbit with a poet's flair,
Writes sonnets in the evening air.
While turtles recite their ages old,
Claiming wisdom that's pure gold.

The clouds above, amused and bright,
Cast shadows on this joyous sight.
In every crevice, laughter spills,
Creating magic with fabled thrills.

When raindrops fall like jesters' glee,
The ground erupts in jubilee.
In this world where silliness flies,
Imagination cannot disguise!

## Nature's Written Tongue

In gardens where the daisies dance,
The bees are buzzing, taking their chance.
With petals penned in colors bright,
They scribble laughter in morning light.

The worms compose a wiggly tune,
While crickets play their strings at noon.
Each leaf a page, each twig a verse,
A nature novel, both strange and terse.

The raindrops laugh, a clumsy jest,
As puddles form in their wet quest.
With muddy boots and splashes wide,
The tales of puddles cannot hide.

In every rustle, in every sigh,
The whispers of the wild pass by.
They weave a story, laugh and sing,
In this madcap world, the joy they bring.

## The Palette of the Past

Oh, the colors that the oak trees wear,
A painter's dream, beyond compare.
Each leaf a brushstroke, bold and free,
Creating scenes for all to see.

The tulips laugh in hues so bright,
In a floral riot, pure delight.
They chat in shades, from red to blue,
Confessing secrets, old and new.

The crows, in coats of midnight grace,
Caw out stories, a feathered race.
With squawks and flaps, they share their lore,
A raucous gaggle shouting more!

And in the dusk, as shadows play,
The colors fade, but still they'll stay.
For nature's palette never stops,
It paints the past, in joyous crops.

## In Earth's Gentle Hands

With a shovel's thrust and a little cheer,
The gardener digs and finds what's dear.
Among the roots where gnomes might dwell,
Old secrets whisper, 'Oh, do tell!'

The dandelions, with their cheeky flair,
Rejoice in sun like they don't care.
'We're wild and free!' they gleefully sing,
With golden crowns, they're the true kings.

The ants form lines, a bustling crew,
Marching in patterns like they always do.
While beetles brag about their might,
In this underground, they reign outright.

And as the sun begins to set,
The critters scurry, a brave duet.
In earth's embrace, they find their fun,
A merry party, until they're done.

## Crescendo of the Canopy

The branches sway in a leafy waltz,
As squirrels chatter, it's never their fault.
With acorn tales and playful tricks,
They jump around, in this leafy mix.

The flowers nod, in a polka-dot dress,
While butterflies glide with grace and finesse.
With every flap, a story flies,
Of sugary treats and sunny skies.

The wind joins in, a gusty laugh,
Tickling the leaves, playing the half.
As shadows stretch and evening falls,
Nature echoes, through sprawling halls.

In the twilight, as creatures hum,
Their laughter lingers, a sweet strum.
The trees uplift their leafy song,
In this grand play, where we all belong.

## **The Harvest of Thought**

In gardens where ideas sprout,
We laugh at weeds that twist about.
The carrots dance, the cabbages sing,
What joy you find in a sprouting thing.

With watering cans that spill the jest,
We plant our dreams where they'll do best.
The radishes joke, the peas tell a tale,
In the patch of laughter, we never fail.

Each seed a chuckle, each root a grin,
The scarecrow's humor makes us all spin.
When harvest comes, the jokes take flight,
We feast on laughter, what a delight!

So dig in deep, let the giggles flow,
In this merry patch, watch us grow.
With every tickle from the ground below,
Our minds take flight, in jovial glow.

## Echoes in the Dirt

Beneath the grass, the giggles hum,
Echoes of laughter, oh what fun!
The rabbits share a sly little tease,
While worms wiggle winks beneath the leaves.

Chickens cluck with a cheeky grin,
Tales of the fox, oh where to begin?
The daisies gossip with the breeze,
In this comedy of nature, we find our ease.

The ants march on with silly pride,
Planning their picnic, full of inside.
Each beetle brings a punchline bright,
Jokes in the garden, oh what a sight!

When the sun sets, the giggles remain,
A chorus of chuckles, like soft rain.
With every rustle and every chirp,
The echoes in the earth make me smirk.

## **Melodies of the Deep Earth**

Down below, the creatures play,
In harmony, they laugh all day.
The gophers compose a silly tune,
While moles dance under the watchful moon.

A symphony of chuckles in the ground,
With every pluck, a new joke found.
The earthworms twist in rhythmic cheer,
In this orchestra, there's nothing to fear.

The roots tap dance beneath the dirt,
As flowers giggle in their bright shirt.
Each beetle adds a note to the song,
In this cheerful chorus, we all belong.

So listen close, to the joyful sound,
In the melodies where laughter's found.
From deep within, let your heart resound,
In the music of life, we are all bound.

## **Trowels and Tercets**

With trowels in hand, we dig and dive,
In the muck of mirth, we feel alive.
Each scoop brings laughter, oh what a thrill,
Creating chaos atop the hill.

Three little phrases and a wink,
In this crafting hub, we never sink.
With every plant, a pun to share,
In this patch of glee, with open air.

We toss the dirt, let the laughter fly,
A gardening club with humor nigh.
The daisies chirp, the sunflowers jest,
In our plot of fun, we feel so blessed.

So come along, with joy upturned,
In the art of growth, we've all learned.
With trowels and words, we cultivate cheer,
In the garden of giggles, we hold dear.

## Feelings in the Furrows

In fields where laughter starts to grow,
The plows dance lightly, sweeping low.
Each bump and jiggle makes us cheer,
While crops gossip, that's quite clear.

With each planted seed, a joke unfurls,
They sprout like giggles, twisting swirls.
As carrots snicker, radishes shout,
In this green realm, there's no doubt.

The sun shines bright, a chuckling star,
It teases beans, 'You won't go far!'
While cucumbers wink with greenish grins,
Among the roots, the fun begins.

And as we harvest with joy so grand,
The dirt's our friend, not just the land.
With muddy boots and tales to share,
In laughter's furrows, we find our care.

## Sowing Words

With a shovel dive, we start to play,
Planting tales in a funny way.
Each word a seed, we chuckle and throw,
As giggles sprout, watch the tales grow.

The sun beamed down with a wink so sly,
As we wrote our verses, standing high.
The wind whispered jokes through leafy greens,
While we scribbled rhymes in the morning scenes.

The crows sat laughing, oh what a sight,
At all our antics, morning 'til night.
Their cawing echoing, a comic book line,
As we sowed the punchlines, all in good time.

In rows so neat, our meanings twist,
As the words sprout up, we can't resist.
Harvesting laughter is quite the art,
In the garden of jest, we grow from the heart.

## Reaping Music

With sickles flashing, we dance and sway,
Harvesting tunes at the end of the day.
Each note a fruit, each chord a sprout,
In rhythms of laughter, we spin about.

The drums are made of hollowed beets,
As we clap to the sound of our funny beats.
Violin vines creeping up to the sun,
In this field of mirth, we all are one.

Cornstalks sway to the melodies high,
As melodies tumble from the sky.
With tomatoes jammin' like stars in the night,
Our musical harvest is pure delight.

In the barn, we gather and sing, oh what fun,
Reaping the joy as the day is done.
The echoes of laughter, a vibrant refrain,
In the heart of the harvest, let's dance again.

## The Language of Loam

In the deep of the earth, a chatter so spry,
The worms hold meetings, oh me, oh my!
With roots that listen, they giggle and chat,
In the choir of dirt, imagine that!

The rocks play marbles; it's quite a game,
While ants debate who's the best at the fame.
But watch out for beetles, their jokes are quite strong,
In the language below, you can't go wrong.

Fungi whisper secrets, knitted in lace,
On a quest for puns in this brown, cozy space.
Each leaf a letter, each sprig a line,
In this earthy humor, we find divine.

So let's dig deeper, let's plow the ground,
For in hidden passages, many laughs abound.
The language of nature, a joyous embrace,
In the heart of the earth, we find our place.

## Hidden Lines Beneath Beets

Under the surface, where secrets lie,
Beets tell tales, with mischievous eye.
They pencil in stories, rich and sweet,
With radishes laughing, they'll never admit defeat.

Carrots write letters, all underground,
In the soil where humor is often found.
They giggle together amid the dark bed,
With sweet puns sprouting right over their head.

As the gopher investigates the ground floor,
He finds all the lines, wanting to score.
Beneath the beets, the laughter grows wide,
In this veggie world, all puns we can't hide.

So dig up the riddles and take them to share,
With a side of green beans, metaphorical flair.
In the garden of giggles, we cheerfully find,
The rich, funny tales that nature has lined.

## Chronicles of the Seed

In a tiny husk, a dream does sleep,
The world outside makes plans to creep.
A beetle waltzes, quite in a flap,
While roots entwine in a happy nap.

Sunshine winks, the rain's a surprise,
The waiting sprout peeks with big eyes.
"Am I a flower? Or dinner plate?"
Giggles arise in the harvest fate.

The caterpillar munches with glee,
"I'm just helping! Can't you see?"
Yet every nibble, a dance with fate,
Growing too fast? Oh, what a state!

A squirrel darts past with an acorn in jaw,
"Why're you so green?" "It's the soil's flaw!"
The sprout just chuckles, as bold as a weed,
"Let's flip the script, I'm the star, yes indeed!"

## The Darkest Comedy of Growth

A seedling dreams beneath the dirt,
"Why's my neighbor such a flirt?"
A sunflower preens, so tall and proud,
"Don't ask," says the bean, "it's just her crowd."

The radish frets, "I think I'm late,"
"Chill out!" cries the kale, "You're just first rate!"
Yet as they bicker, rain starts to pour,
"Quick! Hide the gossip under the floor!"

A worm rolls through, all slick and sly,
"Down your roots, my friends, or you'll dry!"
They roll their eyes, "Get lost, oh squirmy,
We're growing here, not being a germy!"

But under the sun with laughter they wrangle,
"I'll be a carrot!" "I want to dangle!"
Through layers deep, their humor flows,
In this comedy of growth, everyone grows!

## Verses in Every Grain

A speck of dust tells a tale so grand,
With giggles and whispers from grainy land.
"Who knew we could sprout, just like a joke?"
Laughter erupts as the old oak spoke.

"Hey look!" shouts a sprout, "I can dance!"
"Bet you can't twirl!" "Oh, give me a chance!"
The petals join in, a color parade,
Each little hop, no effort to trade.

In this field, puns bloom like daisies,
And broccoli dreams of outrageous phrases.
"Just plant me deep, watch my humor rise,
I promise you laughs with no disguise!"

As rain sings down in playful drops,
Each kernel chuckles, a joke that pops.
So come, my friends, in this plot we reign,
Life's too short for anything mundane!

## Symphonies of the Succulent

A cactus stands with pride on the shelf,
With snickers and giggles, the jester itself.
"Prickly yet charming, what a delight!"
"Oh please, just a pinch, don't start a fight!"

The succulents sway to a swingy beat,
With roots in the rhythm, a funny feat.
"Is it me or the breeze that's making us dance?"
"Both, my dear friend, let's seize the chance!"

A pot on the windowsill sings to the bee,
"Hey there, little buzz, come share some tea!"
"Not now, my friend, I'm on a sweet quest,"
"Then buzz off, and bring back what's best!"

As sunshine streams, the laughter rises,
In this garden of jokes, there're no surprises.
Together they thrive, in humor and glee,
The symphonies grow, wild and free!

## Echoes of the Garden

In the plot where the carrots roar,
A rabbit sings, 'I want more!'
Tomatoes dance with great delight,
While onions giggle out of sight.

Dandelions wear their funny hats,
As bees buzz by with gossip chats.
The sunflowers strike a silly pose,
Debating if they're pros or foes.

The worms hold court beneath the ground,
Claiming they are quite profound.
With every dig, they tell a joke,
The punch in the soil, they provoke.

In this place where fun takes root,
Even the nettles try to loot.
Every sprout has a wacky spin,
While underfoot, the laughter's din.

## **Stanzas in the Dark**

When the twilight whispers low,
Chickens strut with quite a show.
They cluck in rhymes, a silly feat,
Under moonlight, they tap their feet.

The crickets play their nightly song,
While fireflies jiggle all night long.
In shadowed nooks where laughter grows,
The night blooms with comedic prose.

In the dark, the mischief thrives,
Even the patty-pans come alive.
The pumpkins grinning, oh so wide,
At every scary guest outside.

So hush, dear garden, take a rest,
Tomorrow brings another jest.
A show of nature, laughs abound,
Where humor in the dark is found.

## Cradle of the Green

In the cradle where veggies play,
Radishes shout, 'Who's lost today?'
With peas in pods that giggle and grin,
While lettuce leaves cheer, 'Let's begin!'

A cabbage rolls in like a champ,
Declaring, 'I'm the garden's lamp!'
Garlic laughs with a stinky breath,
Saying, 'I thrive, even in death!'

The herbs hold their council with flair,
Mint cracks jokes, 'I'm fresh, I swear!'
Basil points out the tomato's blush,
While beet greens compete in a rush.

Each sprig and root's a merry sight,
In this cradle where joys take flight.
Life's a riot in each little seed,
Where laughter and green are guaranteed.

## **Tangled Verses**

In tangled rows, the radishes speak,
While carrots surprise with a quirky streak.
Beets whisper gossip, bold and spry,
And cabbages giggle as they pass by.

As sprouts intertwine in a silly race,
Zucchini rolls with a laugh on its face.
Corn cackles loud, its height a boast,
While peas get tangled, loving the roast.

The herbs weave jokes into the breeze,
With rosemary tickling the buzzing bees.
Garlic's puns are pungently ripe,
As sass fills the air, oh, what a type!

So here in this mix, the fun never ends,
In the playful embrace that nature lends.
A tapestry of laughter so fine,
Where every root has a punchline.

## From Ashes to Green

A cactus wore a fancy dress,
Swaying proudly in the mess.
Roots, they giggle, twirl around,
While worms dance under ground.

A potato dreams of being fries,
Winks to carrots, such a prize!
While daisies gossip, bold and spry,
Earthworms chuckle, oh my, my!

On Tuesday grass decided to sing,
But ended up stuck under a swing.
Bees kept buzzing, full of charm,
And ants marched by with none alarm.

Yet from ashes, sprouts do rise,
Sprinkled with laughter, full of surprise.
In this garden, silly and bright,
Nature's jest brings pure delight.

## The Fertile Silence

In the quiet of the rich ground,
Dandelions make silly sounds.
They giggle when the raindrops fall,
And mushrooms play hide and seek, what a ball!

Tadpoles wear their tiny hats,
While crickets practice acrobat stats.
The breeze jumps in with tickly glee,
Announcing, 'It's time for tea!'

A cabbage tried to do a jig,
Tangled in a leafy wig.
Frogs burst into fits of glee,
As the ground shook with jubilee.

Under the moon, shadows prance,
While night critters join the dance.
Laughter echoes, soft and loud,
In the fertile hush, we're all so proud.

## Rhymes of Rich Earth

A worm recited poetry sweet,
While the daisies tapped their feet.
But grass got jealous and said, 'Oh no,'
She's got rhymes, but can't steal the show!

Ants, they chorused, 'We're the best!"
As they marched upon their quest.
With tiny trumpets, they made a fuss,
And even the mole joined the chorus thus.

A radish whispered, 'Do you dare?'
While turnips giggled, shaking everywhere.
Roses chimed in with a cheeky rhyme,
While potatoes changed their party time.

In the poetry of the ground below,
Lies laughter that continues to flow.
With every sprout that bursts on through,
Nature composes a funny debut.

## Underfoot Lullabies

Underfoot, where dreams take flight,
Wiggly worms sing through the night.
Little roots tell tales so grand,
As they tickle soft soil and sand.

A beetle plays the tambourine,
While flowers sway, looking keen.
Frogs croak out a serenade,
And fireflies dance, as if they've stayed.

'What's that rustle?' a bunny will say,
'Probably just the mulberry's sway!'
And ants agree with a tiny cheer,
While moles giggle, hiding near.

The world beneath is a playful gig,
As laughter grows, both big and sprig.
In the lullabies of earth's embrace,
Nature's humor finds its place.

## The Language of Leaves

Whispers in green, what's the scoop?
A leaf told a joke, made the branches droop.
Chirping of crickets joined in the fun,
They laughed so hard, the sun started to run.

Squirrels giggled, gathering pretzels so fine,
As acorns clapped, in a merry design.
What's the punchline? Oh, they loved the tease,
Leaves rolled on the ground, laughing with ease.

Petals chimed in, they knew all the quirks,
With funky dance moves, they painted with jerks.
A breeze swayed along, joining the cheer,
Nature's great jesters, bringing joy near!

In this comedy club under skies bright and vast,
Each creature's laughter echoed, a spell they cast.
They all play a part, in this leafy charade,
Where humor and life, in harmony, invade.

# Chronicles of Clay

Mud pies for breakfast, oh what a treat!
With splashes and giggles beneath tiny feet.
The ground had a story of untold delight,
Each squishy adventure made everything right.

Digging for treasure, what a wild dream!
Finding old sneakers, or so it would seem.
The laughter erupted as toes touched the goo,
In this messy kingdom, where dreams come true.

Chasing the worms, those wigglers of cheer,
Declaring them pets, come hold them, my dear!
They slither and slide, with smiles on their face,
In this muddy realm, at a delightful pace.

The tales of the earth are funny and grand,
A festival of joy led by nature's hand.
With clay-covered giggles, we dance with the day,
In the land of the goofy, we frolic and play.

## Unveiling the Depths

Beneath the surface, what secrets reside?
Funny little critters come out for a ride.
They jive with the roots, in a grand, silly tune,
Making mischief below, under the light of the moon.

Rabbits hold meetings, with turtles so wise,
Swapping their stories, and tired old lies.
"Did you hear about Benny, who got stuck in the mud?"
They roared with laughter, "What a goofy dud!"

A mole popped up, with a top hat and flair,
"Let's throw a shindig, invite everyone there!"
Earthworms were sent, with invitations galore,
To a wormy soirée, we cannot ignore.

Finally, the night with stars shining bright,
Creatures of all kinds joined in the delight.
With laughter and dancing, who knew they could leap?
Unveiling the charm, where the depths make you peep!

## Tales from the Turf

Once upon a time, grass had a wish,
To grow a big mustache, just like a fish.
They giggled and chuckled as weeds cheered them on,
A turf party brewed, from dusk until dawn.

Bouncing atop, a frog wearing a crown,
Recited the tales that made everyone frown.
"Hop on the beat!" shouted crickets so spry,
As blades wiggled along, under one silly sky.

Dandelions danced, all decked out in gold,
Claiming they're stars, being bold and so old.
Each puff of their seeds, tossed high in the air,
In their cloud of laughter, nothing could compare.

The lawn held secrets, laughs thick like stew,
Every patch had a story, a giggle or two.
From the roots of the charm to the tips of the blades,
In this realm of mischief, joy never fades.

## The Textured Terrain

In the garden where gnomes can prance,
They plot while rabbits steal a glance.
Worms wiggle, dancing in the dark,
An earthworm's rumble, oh what a lark!

Patches of clover, a clumsy array,
A patchwork quilt on display.
With each little sprout, laughter takes flight,
Green-thumbed mischief from morning to night.

The daisies giggle, they think they're grand,
While dandelions make mischief, oh so unplanned.
Their fluffy seeds, like thoughts in the air,
A sneeze, a joke, it's a wild affair!

In this land of whimsical bloom,
Nature's folly fills every room.
So grab a trowel, don't be shy,
Join in the fun, let your laughter fly!

## **Hideaway of Harmonies**

In the thicket, where critters hum,
A raccoon sneaks in, oh what a bum!
The frogs croak out a serenade,
While crickets claim the grand parade.

A squirrel juggles acorns with flair,
As sparrows gossip without a care.
The cool breeze whistles, tunes intertwine,
Creating a symphony that's simply divine.

Beneath the shade, laughter seeds sprout,
Inviting all critters, come join the bout!
With rustling leaves birthing giggles anew,
In this merry hideaway, hearts accrue.

Nature's choir, a comical blend,
Where all are welcome, and fun won't end.
So find a spot, and turn up the cheer,
In the harmony of laughter, you'll find good cheer!

## **Panoply of the Pasture**

In the field where the clovers sway,
A donkey tells tales of a glorious day.
Cows start mooing in tones quite absurd,
As sheep share secrets, not one word heard.

The butterflies dance with grace so grand,
While goats defy gravity, oh what a stand!
With every hoof print, a new joke devised,
It's comedy central, oh so well-prized.

Beneath the sun, the laughter expands,
The dance of daisies, led by tiny hands.
Where every breeze carries jokes on the wing,
In the field of fun, we twirl and sing!

So raise a glass to this merry squad,
Amidst the pasture, where laughter is broad.
Let's belly laugh and revel with glee,
For in this patch, we're all wild and free!

# Chronicles of the Canopy

Up in the branches, where squirrels convene,
They plot playful pranks upon the unseen.
A woodpecker drums, creating a beat,
While laughter echoes from leaf to leafy seat.

The sunbeams tickle the critters below,
As owls share riddles in their wise, hoot show.
A sloth thinks he's quick, but oh what a joke!
The monkeys tease him, their laughter bespoke.

Twisting vines tell tales of daring escapes,
Where chameleons change into silly shapes.
In this canopy circus, the air's filled with cheer,
A world where giggles happen year after year.

So raise your voice to the creatures so spry,
In this green storytelling, let laughter fly high.
For every leaf holds a story untold,
In the chronicles of green, let joy unfold!

## A Symphony of Sprouts

In gardens where the veggies dance,
They take their chance, they twist and prance.
A cabbage waltzes with delight,
While carrots sing all through the night.

The radishes, they cheer and shout,
'Come join the fun, don't be a rout!'
A beet in shades of crimson red,
Says, 'Let's party, let's be fed!'

The lettuce heads do nod their green,
In unison, they share the scene.
As critters sneak to join the spree,
Even worms groove beneath the lea.

So grab a fork, let's make some noise,
These veggies have such lively joys!
With every crunch, a burst of glee,
In this oddball plant jubilee.

## The Richness Beneath My Feet

In gardens where the treasures hide,
Each little burrow, quite the ride.
The ants parade, they march in line,
Declaring victory for their kind.

The dust bunnies play their tricks;
They make the soil dance and mix.
While grumpy moles, with tiny shovels,
Dig tunnels that cause all sorts of troubles.

Earthworms wiggle, wiggle, wiggle,
While gophers try a sneaky giggle.
A tangle of roots, a party scene,
With radishes plotting how to glean.

So squash the myths, embrace the mess,
The ground below's a vibrant fest.
With every turn, beneath the ground,
A comedy of life is found.

## Celebrating the Underdog

In every patch, a hero waits,
Not all are stars, but still have traits.
The lesser greens, quite underrated,
Their quirky laughs are celebrated.

The broccoli, with its frilly head,
Says, 'Don't forget the seeds we spread!'
While Brussels sprouts, with tiny pride,
Declare, 'We've got our fans worldwide!'

The chard is bold, with colors bright,
Sassier than greens, ready to fight.
From tiny peas, who strive for fame,
To rogue radishes, all play the game.

So raise a glass, let's toast the twig,
To all the roots that dance a jig.
For in this patch, both big and small,
The underdogs shall stand up tall.

## **Tides of Green**

Beneath the surface, pulses swell,
A rhythm where the echoes dwell.
The sprouts will sway, the leaves will swirl,
As life beneath begins to twirl.

A concert held with wormy friends,
They wiggle through, where laughter blends.
The daisies whisper, 'Shh, be still!'
While creeping vines take over the hill.

The seedlings beckon, 'Don't be shy,
Join in the fun, we'll all get high!'
With dandelions, bold and bright,
They scatter seeds with sheer delight.

In every patch, the green waves rise,
A silly splash beneath the skies.
So join the dance, the sprout-filled spree,
In this wild world of jubilee.

## **Green Tapestry Unfurled**


In a patch of muck, a worm took a dive,
Wiggling around, feeling oh so alive.
A sprinkle of rain, a mushroom's delight,
Growing the wrong way, what a funny sight!

Ants marching along with crumbs in their suit,
Chasing down snacks like a tiny old brute.
They stumble and bumble, they tango and spin,
In this wild dance, there's no chance to win!

The grass wears a crown made of jagged old weeds,
Each blade pens a tale in the soil's dim reads.
With giggles from daisies in bright yellow hues,
They gossip 'bout beetles in fancy new shoes!

The sun winks at roots through a wispy old cloud,
Plants whisper secrets, all bundled and loud.
In this playful realm where the odd critters roam,
Even the thorns wear a smile-like a comb!

# Ballads of Buried Life

In the murky depths, a potato sings,
Jubilant and plump, just waiting for springs.
With gnarly old spuds, their dreams take their flight,
Dancing around in the cool moonlight!

A carrot debates with a pompous old turnip,
"I'm longer than you; you're just a short sermon!"
While parsnips chuckle, lying low in the ground,
In their rooty debates, no winner is found.

A gopher with style burrows away with a flair,
Rockin' a top hat, filled with powdered air.
He surveys his realm, with grins all around,
Declaring, "I'm king of this underground town!"

And when night hits, the critters all scheme,
In the darkness, they plot, and they dream.
A banquet of dirt, oh what a grand feast,
With laughter and joy, they dance like a beast!

## Nature's Hidden Lyrics

Beneath the surface, a chorus abounds,
Frogs croak in rhythm, creating strange sounds.
A snail plays a tune on its shiny new shell,
While a mole hums softly, wishing one well.

The roots know the gossip of flowers above,
Whispering tales of their unending love.
A daisy blushes, a rose rolls its eyes,
In this garden so crafty, no truth wears a disguise!

Mice write their ballads on leaves soft and green,
Each note a delight, though nobody's seen.
In their lyrical world, with pure silly grace,
They twirl and they leap, their boots full of haste!

While the bugs laugh and chatter, united in song,
Reminding the flowers, "You all just belong!"
And under the moon, with a twinkle and twang,
The melody rises, then plops with a clang!

## In the Loam's Lull

In shadows so cozy, a bug takes a nap,
Dreaming of journeys in a leaf-covered map.
With dandelion fluff, as a fluffy warm quilt,
He snoozes away, quite the fabled hillside!

The morning dew sparkles like jewels in the sun,
While a ladybug boasts, "I'm the very best one!"
With polka dot style and a wink of its eye,
It struts on the path, oh so smugly spry!

The mushrooms decide to throw parties at night,
With dancing and laughter, what a glorious sight!
With toadstools and roots all in jolly array,
They revel in mirth 'til the break of the day!

With crickets all chirping their tunes neat and fine,
It's nature's grand echo, a silly design.
Though some might just frown at the ruckus and cheer,
In the loam's lively world, there's no need for fear!

www.ingramcontent.com/pod-product-compliance
Lightning Source LLC
Chambersburg PA
CBHW072146200426
43209CB00051B/801